Bible Application

Puppet Skits Kids Can Do

24 Quick and Easy Scripts for Ages 8 to 12

PEGGY BRADSHAW & DEBBIE FREEMAN

STANDARD PUBLISHING

Cincinnati, Ohio

Edited by Theresa C. Hayes
Cover and inside design by Diana Walters

All Scripture quotations, unless otherwise indicated, are quoted from the International Children's Bible, New Century Version, copyright © 1986, 1988 by Word Publishing, Dallas, Texas, 75039. Used by permission.

Standard Publishing, Cincinnati, Ohio.
A division of Standex International Corporation.

ISBN 0-7847-1150-X
© 2000 Standard Publishing
All rights reserved
Printed in the United States of America

All skits are reproducible for ministry purposes only—not for resale.

07 06 05 04 03 02 01 00   5 4 3 2 1

We are extremely thankful to our Lord
and Savior, Jesus Christ,
for the opportunity to write this book.
It is our prayer that through it,
he will reveal himself to many children.
All praise and glory belong to him.

Peggy Bradshaw and Debbie Freeman

Contents

Introduction

Bible Application Puppet Skits Kids Can Do is an easy-to-use children's ministry resource designed to help teach children important Bible themes and concepts. Each puppet skit takes minimal planning and rehearsal, and many skits can involve your entire group. The following are tips that will enable you to present the puppet skits with ease.

Puppets

You will need to have on hand two boy puppets and two girl puppets.

These four puppets can perform all the puppet skits in this book just by adding a few easy costumes and props. See the appendix for a quick, simple, no-sewing-necessary pattern for a biblical costume.

Puppet Stages

If you do not have a puppet stage available, you can easily improvise.

- Turn a table on its side and drape material over the table. Puppeteers can sit on the floor behind the table.

- A large cardboard box, such as a refrigerator box, can become a stage by cutting a square opening in the box as the stage opening. These boxes can be obtained from appliance stores fairly easily.

- A tension curtain rod can be placed in a doorway with a curtain on it. The puppeteers will be out side the door and the audience will be inside the room. If this method is used, the puppeteers must speak very loudly so that their voices will carry into the room.

Sign Puppeteers

Some of the puppet skits require a puppeteer to hold a sign. These signs are used to prompt the audience or emphasize a particular point in the skit. This also gives some of your shier children a chance to perform without having to speak. Most of the signs should be attached to sticks so that they can "dance" or move around instead of just being held up for the audience to see. The sign puppeteers should practice with the other puppeteers.

Props

The props should be made according to the size of the stage and puppets. Most of the props are made with common materials that you may have on hand. If you have artistic children in your group, they may want to make the props themselves.

Two exceptions are the baseball cap and sunglasses for the cheers. You can use a baseball cap and sunglasses made for babies. If they are a little too big, it will add humor to the skit.

Preparation

Some skits require audience participation. When advised, you will have to let the audience know that they are to respond to the signs or to the puppets' inquiries.

Scripts

You may reproduce the scripts so that the puppeteers can take them home to practice.

You will also want a copy of the front and back side of the script for each puppeteer, so that the pages may be taped to the back of the stage for easy reading. You may want to highlight each puppeteer's part in a different color.

Scripts can also be recorded onto an audio cassette. The cassette is then played during the show as the puppets "lip-sync" to the cassette. This is useful if the children have difficulty in keeping the puppets moving and "acting" while they are reading the lines from the script.

Additional Tips for Puppeteers

Have children practice with the puppet with which they are going to perform. They need to practice moving the puppet's mouth in time with the words that they are speaking. The puppet will be lip-syncing the puppeteer's words. Remind the children to bend at the wrist and hold their thumbs down so that the puppet is looking at the audience or other puppets. A big mistake for most beginners is that the puppet seems to be staring at the ceiling. Puppet character voices may be tried by the children. However, they must be able to be heard by the audience and they must be able to sustain the character voice throughout the skit.

The children should also practice making the puppet "act." The more a puppet moves its head and arms or body while talking, the more it will hold the audience's attention. The puppets should look as though they are "walking" as they enter instead of just appearing or popping onto the stage. A small up and down motion will give them the appearance of walking.

Have the children practice in front of a mirror with the puppets and props. They should look only at their puppet in the mirror. Have them ask, "Do the puppet's movements seem real according to what is happening in the skit?" After they have practiced in front of a mirror, have them rehearse behind the stage. When the children become used to handling the puppets, less practice time will be involved.

Puppet Ministry for Children

We have found that puppets are a good way to help shy children grow. These children may not feel comfortable participating in other outgoing activities but will feel at ease being behind stage and letting the puppets do their "acting." They may want to start out by being a sign puppeteer. However, with encouragement and praise, you will help build their confidence enough so that they will want to perform with a puppet that has a speaking part.

For outgoing children, puppets can be a wonderful release of creativity as they try to make their puppets come alive in the skit.

Remember

• Give the children plenty of praise and let them have fun.
• If you are not using the cassette tape method, remind them to speak loudly and clearly.
• Remind them to keep their thumbs down so that the puppet is looking at the audience.
• Remind them to make their puppets move and "act."
• Pray with them before the performance.
• After the performance, give plenty of positive feedback.

Counting the Stars

Scripture: Psalm 19:1-4

Characters: Kailyn, Katie

Costumes/Props
- Modern clothing
- Black fabric to drape over the puppet stage to give it the appearance of night

— Script —

Kailyn enters and looks up at the sky. She points and begins to count slowly.

Kailyn: One, two, three, four, five, six . . . *[continues counting as Katie enters].*

Katie: *[enters and looks at Kailyn, then at the sky, then at Kailyn, and then at the sky again]* Hey, Kailyn!

Kailyn: *[continues counting]* . . . twelve, thirteen, fourteen . . . *[keeps pointing and counting].*

Katie: *[looks back and forth between Kailyn and the sky, then calls loudly]* Hey, Kailyn?!

Kailyn: *[continues to slowly count]* . . . twenty, twenty-one, twenty-two . . .

Katie: *[taps Kailyn on shoulder and shouts]* KAILYN!

Kailyn: Twenty . . . twenty . . . twenty? Oh, rats! *[Turns to Katie disgustedly.]* Now look what you've done! I've lost my place. What do you want, Katie?

Katie: Oh, I was just wondering what you are doing.

Kailyn: What does it look like I'm doing? I'm counting—and you made me lose count!

Katie: Oh. Sorry about that.

Kailyn: *[turns her back to Katie and points to the sky and starts counting again]* One, two, three, four, five . . . *[continues counting].*

Katie: *[looks back and forth between Kailyn and the sky]* Kailyn?

Kailyn stops counting but continues pointing at the sky.

Katie: [taps Kailyn on the shoulder again] Hey, is there anybody in there?

Kailyn: [continues to point at the sky as she answers] What?!

Katie: What are you counting?

Kailyn: I am trying to count the stars. Twelve, thirteen, fourteen, fifteen . . .

Katie: Ahem! . . . Excuse me, Kailyn?

Kailyn: [puts her hand down and turns to Katie with a big sigh] What, Katie?

Katie: Well, I hate to ask this, but why are you counting stars?

Kailyn: I am trying to count them because I read on the Internet that we can see almost 3,000 stars without binoculars. I want to see if it's true. [Starts counting again.] One, two, three, four . . .

Katie: [looks up at sky] The stars sure are beautiful, aren't they?

Kailyn: [stops counting but continues to look up] Yeah, they sure are.

Katie: And just think, God made every single one of them. [Points to the sky.] He made that one, and that one, and that one over there. [Pause.] There are millions of stars in our galaxy, you know. And no one really knows how many other galaxies there are—maybe billions. And God made each and every one of them.

Both girls continue looking up.

Kailyn: Billions?

Katie: Yeah. Want me to help you count them?

Kailyn: No, let's just admire them.

Digging Deeper

What part of God's creation seems most awesome to you?

Every time scientists develop a stronger telescope, they discover more stars. What does this tell you about God's power?

Is it more important to be able to see and count the stars, or to appreciate them?

Headlight Smile

Scripture: Genesis 28, 35

Characters: Jason, Jarod, Keisha, one puppeteer to hold sign

Costumes/Props
• Modern clothing
• Small paper bag to attach to hand of Jarod
• Sign saying "God's Promises, Guaranteed for Eternity"

———— Script ————

Jason enters from the left. Keisha and Jarod enter from the right. Jarod is carrying a paper bag.

Jason: There you are. Did you get your yo-yo?

Jarod: Nope.

Jason: Why not? You both worked hard for the money to buy one.

Keisha: We found something better!

Jason: You did?

**Jarod &
Keisha:**   HEADLIGHT TOOTHPASTE!!

Jason: Toothpaste? You bought toothpaste instead of a super-duper, shazam, glow-in-the-dark, siren-blaring yo-yo?

Jarod: Yeah, and wait till you hear what it does!

Jason: Does it glow in the dark or make sounds like a siren?

Keisha: No, silly.

Jason: Then why did you buy it?

Jarod :   Well, we were on our way to the toy department and there it was, a big beautiful sign. It said, "BUY HEADLIGHT TOOTHPASTE!"

Jason: So you bought it just because a sign said to?

Keisha: But wait, you haven't heard the promise. The sign said, "GUARANTEED TO MAKE YOUR TEETH AS WHITE AS A CAR'S HEADLIGHT, AND MAKE YOUR LIFE RICHER!"

Jason: But I thought you wanted a yo-yo, not headlight teeth.

Jarod: Don't you get it?

Jason: I guess not.

Jarod: The sign promised our life would be richer—

Keisha: —so we'll be able to buy all the yo-yos we want!

Jason: You believe toothpaste can do that?

Keisha: Sure, the sign guaranteed it, and a guarantee is a promise.

Jason: Look you guys, the makers of that toothpaste weren't promising you'd get money. And besides, you can't believe everything you see in an advertisement.

Jarod: You can't?

Keisha: Then what can you believe?

Jason: You can believe the promises of God, because he always keeps his promises and does what he says he will do.

Jarod: Well, this was a waste [holds up bag].

Keisha: Yeah, the only thing we'll get is a headlight smile.

Jason: And maybe not even that! [All exit.]

Sign: "God's Promises, Guaranteed for Eternity"

Digging Deeper

Have you ever seen a TV commercial that made a toy look really great, but when you got the toy, it wasn't nearly as great? What does this tell you about commercials?

The Bible tells us that it is impossible for God to lie (Hebrews 6:18) and that Jesus came into this world to tell us the truth (John 18:37). How does this make you feel about the promises of God?

When you are hurt because someone has lied to you, does it help to remember that God will always love you and always be with you?

Bag of Worries

Scripture: Psalm 55:22

Characters: Lori, Lynn, Lou

Costumes/Props
- Modern clothing
- Paper bag (fill bag with newspapers and stones to make it look heavy). Label the bag "Worries."
- Wad three brown bags into rock shapes. Put a label on each: "Grades," "Looks," "Friends."

Preparation
Tape the paper rocks to the top edge of the stage.
Attach the paper bag of rocks to one of the girl puppet's hands.

Script

Scene opens with Lori carrying paper bag of rocks. She walks in slowly as though bag is very heavy.

Lori: This is getting so heavy. I've been carrying it for such a long time.

Lynn: *[enters from left]* Hey, Lori, what ya' got in the bag?

Lori: Lots and lots of heavy worries. They are pulling me down like a bag of rocks.

Lynn: Well, here, let me help. *[Points to "Grades" rock on stage.]* Oh, look! You missed one over here.

Lori: I know. Everywhere I look there are more. Oh, no! Grades! I think I flunked the math test *[big sigh]*.

Lynn: Here's another one. *[Points to "Looks" rock.]*

Lori: I wish I was taller and had hair like Julie. She's so pretty. *[Sighs.]*

Lynn: Oh, look! You missed this one over here. *[Points to "Friends" rock.]* But I don't know why anyone would worry about friends—I have lots of them!

Lori: *[sadly]* Yeah, I know.

Lynn: Well, I'm glad I could be of help. See ya' later *[exits]*.

Lori: *[weakly]* Bye . . . . *[walks slowly over to the rocks and looks at them one by one, sighing].* I am just so tired of carrying this heavy burden. I don't know how much longer I can do this.

Lou: *[enters from right]* Hi, Lori!

Lori: *[sadly]* Oh, hi, Lou.

Lou: Lori, you look really tired and worried. Let me help you with that bag.

Lori: *[afraid and pleading]* No, please don't put any more rocks in it!

Lou: Lori, I would never do that. I want to help you.

Lori: But shouldn't I be able to handle this by myself?

Lou: No! Not you, or anybody else! God wants us to give all of our worries to him. You don't need to worry about problems in your life because God has promised to take care of us. *[Puts his hand out to help carry the bag.]* Come on, let's go pray.

They exit together.

Digging Deeper ━━━━━━━━━━━━━━━━━━━

When you see a friend who is worried about something, what can you do to help?

When you are worried about something, what should you do?

God speaks to us in many ways to help us with our problems. What are some of these ways?

Sheep Talk

Scripture: John 1:14, 18

Characters: Joel, Hannah, one puppeteer for sign

Costumes/Props:
- A shepherd's staff made from cardboard
- Two shepherds' headdresses (scraps of material tied with string around puppet heads)
- Prompt sign on a stick: "BAA!"
- Optional shepherds' robes (See appendix for pattern.)

Preparation:
Attach the staff to Joel's hand and put the headdresses on both puppets. Ask audience to baa like sheep when the sign appears. Sign remains behind stage until time to appear.

Script

Joel:	*[enters and looks at audience]* Good morning, my woolly little sheep! Are you ready to begin? Let's have our morning lesson, OK? Perk up your woolly ears. Ready? . . . SPEAK!
Sign:	"BAA!" *[Audience responds, sign exits.]*
Joel:	Very good! You've been practicing!
Hannah:	*[runs in, speaks urgently]* Joel! I have something to tell you!
Joel:	*[interrupts]* Oh, wait, Hannah! I have something to show you.
Hannah:	But Joel, this is important!
Joel:	So's this! Just watch! OK, woolly friends, do your stuff! . . . SPEAK!
Sign:	"BAA!" *[Audience responds, sign exits.]*
Joel:	See Hannah, we can talk to each other!
Hannah:	Wow, Joel, that's incredible! But I ran all the way here to tell you there's a big storm coming. Papa says to move the sheep to safety.
Joel:	No, problem! . . . Line up, guys.
Sign:	"BAA!" *[Audience responds, sign exits.]*

Joel:	No, not speak, MOVE!
Sign:	"BAA!" *[Audience responds, sign exits.]*
Hannah:	Come on, Joel, talk to them!
Joel:	I am talking to them . . . Shoo, sheep! . . . Oh, great! Now they're scattering everywhere!
Hannah:	That's not working! Can't you make them understand?
Joel:	I'm trying! Do you have any ideas?
Hannah:	Sorry, Joel, you're the shepherd.
Joel:	*[talks to self]* All right, Joel, think, think, think! . . . Well, Jesus is our Shepherd and he saved us . . . Maybe I'm just not a good shepherd.
Hannah:	But Joel, Jesus became a man to help us understand that he loves us and wants to save us. But you can't become a sheep.
Joel:	Uh-oh! Here comes the rain! Quick, help me, Hannah!

Joel and Hannah exit in opposite directions, calling the sheep.

Both:	Here, sheep! Here, sheep!

Digging Deeper

Hannah was exactly right about Jesus becoming a man so that he could help us understand God better. Why is that so important to us?

A shepherd leads his sheep, and protects them, but is he really able to talk to them? How is our Good Shepherd able to do more for us?

How can we show Jesus that we are thankful that he is our Good Shepherd?

Miracles, Not Magic

Scripture: John 20:30, 31

Characters: Garrett, Shannon

Costumes/Props:
- Modern clothing
- Bandanna or handkerchief attached to Garrett's hand in such a way that he can let go of it

—————— Script ——————

Garrett: *[enters with a bandanna in hands, is practicing saying "Abra-ca-dabra" in different voices]* Abra-ca-dabra! . . . No, ah . . . Abra-ca-dabra! . . . Hmm. . . . How about this? . . . Abra-ca-dabra! That's it! Abra-ca-dabra!

Shannon: *[enters from left]* Hey, Garrett, what ya' doin'?

Garrett: Hi, Shannon! I'm practicing for the talent show at school. Want to see my act?

Shannon: Sure, go ahead.

Garrett: *[clears his throat, speaks in loud voice]* Ahem . . . Ladies and Gentlemen, the Great Gorganzola . . .

Shannon: Gorganzola?

Garrett: *[speaks in regular voice]* Yeah, that's my stage name. *[Returns to other voice.]* The Great Gorganzola will now do his world famous MIRACLE! I will make this ordinary bandanna completely disappear. When I say "Abra-ca-dabra," please shut your eyes. When I count to three, you may open them again. Ready?

Shannon: I guess.

Garrett: Abra-ca-dabra!

Shannon covers her eyes with her hands.

Garrett: *[drops the bandanna on the floor in front of the stage]* One! Two! Three!

Shannon uncovers her eyes.

Garrett: Voilà! The bandanna has completely disappeared. It's a MIRACLE!

Shannon: Hmmm . . . Garrett, your trick was great. But it wasn't a miracle.

Garrett: Sure it was. I made the bandanna disappear, didn't I?
Shannon: Well, sort of, but it was just a magic trick, not a miracle.

Garrett: What do you mean?

Shannon: Magic is just a trick to fool people. Anyone can do a magic trick. But there is only one person who can perform miracles.

Garrett: Really? Is he a great magician?

Shannon: No, he is God's Son. He is the one and only great, miracle-working, Jesus.

Garrett: You mean Jesus does tricks?

Shannon: No, Garrett, miracles are not tricks.

Garrett: So, my act is just a great magic trick?

Shannon: Well, maybe not so great—*[looks down at the floor]* you dropped your bandanna.

Both exit.

Digging Deeper

How would you explain the difference between magic tricks and miracles?

A miracle is defined as an event that breaks the laws of nature. Why is Jesus able to work miracles?

How does it make you feel to know that this same miracle-working Jesus is your personal friend?

Far Out!

Scripture: John 4:1-41

Characters: Pablo, Niki

Preparation: Ask audience to respond when puppet speaks to them.

Script

Pablo and Niki enter together.

Pablo: Hey, Niki, do you want to be in my club?

Niki: Well, what kind of club is it?

Pablo: It's the Far-Out Fifty Friends Club.

Niki: That sounds cool, but do you have to be fifty years old to join?

Pablo: No! Not fifty years old—fifty friends! We'll have fifty members and that's all that we'll let in.

Niki: Cool!

Pablo: And we'll only let people who can whistle be in the club 'cause I just learned to whistle.

Niki: That sounds great! Hey, here are some kids now! Maybe they could be in our club. *[Turns to audience.]* How many of you can whistle? Go ahead and let us hear your whistle! *[Audience responds.]* Umm . . . Pablo, it sounds like some of these kids won't make it in our club. We might have to call it the Far-Out Fifteen Friends Club.

Pablo: Oh, OK! That works. And Niki . . . I was thinking . . . All of our members should be able to touch their tongues up to their noses.

Niki: Huh?

Pablo: Yeah, Far-Out Friends have got to be able to do that.

Niki: *[turns to audience]* OK, of those of you who can whistle, how many of you can touch your nose with your tongue? *[Audience responds.]* Uh, Oh, Pablo! I think we have a problem. Our club is going to be the Far-Out Five Friends Club.

Pablo: Well, I guess that'll be OK. But, Niki, I think our members should be able to wiggle their ears, too.

Niki: *[turns to audience]* OK, how many of you can whistle, touch your tongue to your nose and . . . hey, wait a minute! I can't wiggle my ears!!

Pablo: You can't?

Niki: No!

Pablo: Then how can you be a Far-Out Friend?

Niki: Pablo, we don't have to all look alike and act alike to be friends. Jesus is a friend to all people.

Pablo: You mean our club members don't all have to be the same?

Niki: No. Jesus showed us how to love everyone!

Pablo: So, we don't all have to, ah . . . whistle? *[Tries to whistle but he just blows really hard with no sound.]* My whistle really isn't very good yet. Hey, how about if we start a "Far-Reaching Friends of Jesus Club?"

Niki: Now that's far out!

Digging Deeper

Does God set restrictions on who can come to him?

Why do you think some people judge other people by how they look, or what they can do?

The Bible tells us that people look at the outside of a person, but the Lord looks at the heart (1 Samuel 16:7). How can we learn to care more about what's inside a person than what's outside?

She Doesn't Deserve It!

Scripture: Jonah 1–4

Characters: Jamal, Tasha, Kim

——— Script ———

Tasha and Kim enter from right, laughing. Jamal enters from left, remains on the left side of the stage.

Jamal: Um, Tasha, could I talk to you?

Tasha: Sure, Jamal. *[Both girls move toward Jamal.]*

Jamal: Well, I meant privately! Could I speak to you alone . . . *[nods toward Kim]* without HER?

Tasha: *[scolding voice]* Jamal!

Kim: *[sadly]* Oh . . . OK. I guess I'll see you later. *[Kim exits right, slowly with head down.]*

Jamal: *[with anger]* Tasha, what are you doing?

Tasha: That's easy. I'm talking to you, Jamal. Remember, you said you wanted to talk to me privately?

Jamal: No, not that! I mean, what are you doing with KIM?

Tasha: Oh, she was just telling me some jokes. Say, Jamal, what do the little lambs do before they go to bed?

Jamal: I don't know. What do the little lambs do before they go to bed?

Tasha: They take their b-a-a-a-a-ths. *[Giggles.]*

Jamal: Very funny, Tasha, but what are you doing talking to Kim?

Tasha: I told you, she was telling me jokes. She's really funny.

Jamal: You didn't think she was so funny last week when she made a joke about your hair!

Tasha: *[touches her hair]* Yeah, you're right! That wasn't very funny!

Jamal: Not very funny? It was downright mean!

Tasha: Well, I suppose it wasn't very nice.

Jamal: So?!

Tasha: So what?

Jamal: So, why are you laughing with her today?

Tasha: I told you. It's because she's so funny and . . . and . . .

Jamal: And?

Tasha: And because I forgave her.

Jamal: You forgave her, after what she said? She doesn't deserve to be forgiven!

Tasha: Jamal, I didn't forgive her because she deserved it. I forgave her because it is what Jesus would want me to do.

Jamal: Hmmm . . . *[is quiet for a minute, then calls off stage]* Oh, Kim?

Kim enters with her head down.

Jamal: Kim, I'm sorry for the way I acted. I know it wasn't very nice. Will you forgive me?

Kim: *[perks up]* Sure! Do you want to hear a joke? *[All start to exit.]* Knock! Knock!

Digging Deeper

Have you ever said anything unkind about another person's hair, or clothes, or accent, or abilities? Ever been mean to a brother or sister? Ever smarted off to a parent or a teacher? How would you feel if all of those people had never forgiven you?

Jesus died so that ALL our sins could be forgiven. Since God loves us this much, shouldn't we be able to love others enough to forgive them?

How do you feel when you forgive someone?

No Doubt About It!

Scripture: John 21:1-14

Characters: Peter, Thomas, one puppeteer to hold the signs

Costumes/Props:
- Bible robes (See appendix for suggested pattern.)
- Sign to read "Heard what?"
- Sign to read "Jesus is Alive!"

Preparation: Ask audience to read the signs when they appear.

Script

Thomas and Peter enter together.

Thomas: Hey, Peter, do you think they know? *[Points to audience.]*

Peter: They must have heard.

Thomas: I doubt it.

Peter: Thomas, you doubt everything.

Thomas: Not everything. Go on, ask them!

Peter: OK. *[Turns to audience:]* Have you heard?

Sign: "Heard what?" *[Audience responds. Sign exits.]*

Peter: *[turns to Thomas]* You're right! They haven't heard! Well, we can remedy that! . . . Ready?

Thomas: Ready!

Peter: *(Can be delivered either as a rap or a cheer.)*
I remember it well—it was a Sunday night.
We were sittin' in a room with the doors locked tight.
We were scared and tired and filled with gloom.
Then Jesus walked in—into the room!

Thomas: Well, I wasn't with them in the room that night,
And I couldn't believe they'd seen that sight.

But the Lord knew my heart and he hunted me down.
The very next week he came back to town.

He said, "See my hands, touch my side.
Stop doubting and believe—I am alive."
And now I know Jesus is alive.
I've touched his hands, his feet, his side.

Peter: Then a few days later we were fishin' in the sea,
Tom and me on Lake Galilee.
We fished all night without a single bite,
So we pulled in the nets with the morning light.

Then I saw a man standin' on the shore;
Not just a man—there was something more.
He said, "Throw in your nets on the other side."
And I'm not sure why, but we gave it a try.

Thomas: Next thing you know there were fish everywhere.
Pete was screamin', and jumpin' in the air.
He just couldn't stand it one second more,
So he jumped off the boat and headed for shore.

The rest of us followed, dragging in that boat;
There were so many fish it could barely float.
And there was Jesus cookin' fish and bread.
We saw him alive—risen from the dead!

Both: We've seen him! *(clap, clap)*

Sign: "Jesus is Alive." *[Audience responds. Sign exits.]*

Both: We know that— *(clap, clap)*

Sign: "Jesus is Alive." *[Audience responds. Sign exits.]*

Both: Let's hear it! *(clap, clap)*

Sign: "Jesus is Alive." *[Audience responds. Sign exits.]*

All shout: ALIVE!

Thomas and Peter exit.

Digging Deeper

If you had been one of Jesus' disciples (as Thomas was) and you had watched him die, would it have been hard for you to believe that he was alive again?

Why did Jesus allow so many people to see him alive again before he returned to Heaven? Why didn't he just go straight to Heaven from the tomb?

Why should Jesus' resurrection make us so happy that we shout and cheer and clap our hands?

Fair Sheep

Scripture: Psalm 95:6, 7

Characters: Brian, Bethy (speaks in baby talk), Brett

Script

All three puppets enter together, with Bethy in the middle.

Brian: *[speaks excitedly]* WHOA! I just love the fair. I want to see everything!

Bethy: I wanna see the lambies and eat cotton candy.

Brett: Hey, let's go ride the Dragon's Tail!

Bethy: *[loudly]* I wanna see the lambies!

Brian: Oh, Bethy, you are just like a little lamb.

Bethy: I am?

Brett: You sure are. My Sunday school teacher said that we are all like sheep.

Bethy: *[a little angrily]* What you mean I'm a sheep!?

Brian: Well, sheep like to have their own way.

Bethy: I'm not like that, I just want to see the lambies.

Brett: And they have to be fed.

Bethy: I like cotton candy.

Brian: Don't forget about water—sheep need help when they're thirsty.

Bethy: Yeah, I need help 'cuz I'm too short to reach the drinking fountain.

Brett: They need to be protected from danger, too.

Bethy: You mean like when you hold my hand to cross the street?

Brian: Yes, and sometimes they get lost, like someone else we know *[looks at Bethy]*.

Bethy:	*[hangs her head]* Uh-oh.
Brett:	They just need lots of help from the shepherd.
Bethy:	Shepherd? What's a shepherd?
Brian:	He is the person who loves the sheep and takes care of them.
Brett:	I heard Pastor _____ say that Jesus is our Shepherd.
Bethy:	Jesus loves me!
Brian:	And he takes care of all of us.
Brett:	See, Bethy, we are all like sheep.
Bethy:	Well, I'm NOT going to eat grass!

All three begin to exit.

Brian:	*[as he exits]* How about some cotton candy instead?

Digging Deeper

How many ways can you think of that people are like sheep?

How many ways can you think of that Jesus is our Good Shepherd?

When you are afraid, or lost, or worried, do you remember to ask Jesus for help?

God Is in Control

Scripture: Daniel 4:34, 35

Characters: Abby, Gabby, two puppeteers to handle signs

Costumes/Props:
- Two signs on sticks: "God Is in Control!" and "Give God the Glory!"
- baseball caps (worn backwards) or sunglasses or pompoms

Preparation:
- This skit can be done either as a rap or as a responsive cheer. Dress puppets accordingly.
- Prepare audience to respond on cue to the signs.

———— Script ————

Signs are held below stage, out of sight. Signs "dance" when they appear.

Abby: This is a story to let you know
We're not in charge, God is in control.
He uses men to carry out his plan,
But God is the one in charge, my man.

Gabby: When we get to thinkin' that it's our story,
We forget to stop and give God the glory.
We try on our own to reach the goal;
We forget to say, "God is in control!"

Both: Tell me, what do you know?

Sign: "GOD IS IN CONTROL!" *[Sign exits.]*

Both: And what's the story?

Sign: "GIVE GOD THE GLORY!"

Both: Say, what's the story?

Sign: "GIVE GOD THE GLORY!" *[Sign exits.]*

(You can use this cheer after every verse, if you wish.)

Abby: You know Joseph's story wasn't much to tell,
From standin' in the bottom of an empty well.
His brothers took his coat and threw him in a hole,
But he knew God was in control.

Gabby: Life can look bad and things get smelly
When you're sittin' in the bottom of a big fish belly.
But Jonah cried out to God, you know,
Saying, "I'm not the boss! You're in control!"

Both: Tell me, what do you know?

Sign: "GOD IS IN CONTROL!" [Sign exits.]

Both: And what's the story?

Sign: "GIVE GOD THE GLORY!"

Both: Say, what's the story?

Sign: "GIVE GOD THE GLORY!" [Sign exits.]

Abby: Joseph, Jonah, Esther, Paul,
Daniel, Moses, count them all.
Shadrach, Meshach, Abednego
All knew God was in control.

Gabby: So, if things look bad and things look grim,
Look to Jesus, keep your eyes on him.
Love him with your whole heart, mind, and soul,
'Cause he loves you and he's in control!

Both: Tell me what do you know?

Sign: "GOD IS IN CONTROL!" [Sign exits.]

Both: And what's the story?

Sign: "GIVE GOD THE GLORY!"

Both: Say, what's the story?

Sign: "GIVE GOD THE GLORY!" [Sign exits.]

All: YEAH!

Digging Deeper

Why do you think the Bible tells us about so many people who God rescued from dangerous situations?

Why is it important to remember that God is in control?

What are some ways that you can "give God the glory"?

Scripture: Romans 6:23 (NIV)

Characters: Jimmy, Rhonda, four puppeteers to hold signs

Costumes/Props:
- Small piece of paper for list
- Letters spelling "ETERNAL," each letter on a separate paper

— Script —

Jimmy: *[enters stage right, carrying a list]* Let's see, I'll need to get a fish bowl, some rocks, some turtle food, and a water dish. Then—

Rhonda: *[enters stage left, interrupts Jimmy]* Hey Jimmy, what's going on?

Jimmy: Oh, I'm just getting ready for my turtle.

Rhonda: Your turtle? Are you going to buy a turtle?

Jimmy: Nope. Weren't you listening to Pastor _____ at church last week when he talked about the free turtles?

Rhonda: Free turtles? I must have missed that. I don't remember anything about turtles.

Jimmy: Sure you do. His whole message was about that turtle verse—he read it right from the Bible.

Rhonda: Which verse is that?!

Jimmy: You know! "The gift of God is a turtle life." So I want to be ready when I get my free turtle.

Rhonda: Excuse me, Jimmy, but I think the Scripture that Pastor _____ was talking about is the part of Romans 6:23 that says, "the gift of God is e-ternal life in Christ Jesus our Lord."

Jimmy: Not "a turtle"?

Rhonda: No, "eternal."

Jimmy: So what's e-turtle? Turtles that e-mail each other?

Rhonda: No, Jimmy. The word is e t e r n a l.

Jimmy: Eternal? That's a new word for me. How is it spelled? And what does it mean? *Puppeteer holds up the letter "E."*

Rhonda: Eternal starts with the letter "E," as in endless, or everlasting.

Jimmy: What's next?

Puppeteer holds up the letter "T." (And so on with remaining letters.)

Rhonda: Next comes "T," as in "to infinity and beyond!"

Jimmy: Cool! I think I'm getting the idea!

Rhonda: Next comes another "E," as in eons and eons and eons. Then "R" as in remaining forever.

Jimmy: Let me try! How about "N" for never-ending, and "A" for always?

Rhonda: Good! And the last letter is "L" for a long, long, long, long time!

Jimmy: So the gift of God is endless, everlasting, to infinity and beyond, eons and eons, remaining forever, always, long, long, long, long, eternal life!

Rhonda: Jimmy, I think you've got it!

Jimmy: Wow, that's a lot better than a free turtle!

Puppeteers hold up signs for E T E R N A L as Jimmy and Rhonda exit.

Digging Deeper

How would you explain the word "eternal" to a friend?

When time seems to pass slowly here on earth, it's usually because we're waiting for something good to happen. Will time ever seem slow when we're in Heaven?

Because God is eternal, he has always existed—and always will. How does it make you feel to know that you can spend eternity with God in Heaven?

Waiting

Scripture: Titus 2:11-13

Characters: Monty Mouth, Gimme Moore, Ima Lovely, Jimmy

Costumes/Props:
• Microphone for Monty (lollipop or sucker wrapped in black tape or felt)

Script

Monty: *[newsman enters carrying a microphone]* We interrupt our regularly scheduled program with an important message. This is Monty Mouth, your man on the street. It was just revealed to our sources that people everywhere are waiting. But, the big question is, "What are they waiting for?" Oh, here comes someone now.

Gimme Moore enters from the left.

Monty: Excuse me, Ma'am. What is your name? *[Holds microphone so that she can speak into it.]*

Gimme: My name is Gimme. Gimme Moore.

Monty: Yes, well, Ms. Moore, could you tell us what it is that you're waiting for?

Gimme: That's easy! I'm waiting to win the lottery, then all my troubles will be over. Gotta' run so I can buy more tickets. I hear the lottery is up to 40 million dollars! *[Gimme hurries off to the left.]*

Monty: Thank you, Ms. Moore.

Ima Lovely enters from right.

Monty: Excuse me, Miss?

Ima: *[looks for camera]* OH! Am I on TV? *[Pats hair, leans toward the microphone that Monty is holding.]* Ima Lovely, that's my name. That's I-M-A, L-O-V-E-L-Y.

Monty: Well, Miss Lovely, what is it you're waiting for?

Ima: I'm waiting to become a movie star, and this could be my big break! *[Pats hair and poses.]*

Monty:	I see! *[Turns away from Ima.]* Now, for our next interview . . .
Ima:	*[in disgust]* Well, EXCUSE ME! *[Tromps off stage to the right.]*
Monty:	*[turns and looks around stage]* Now, let me see . . . I need one more person to interview.
Jimmy:	*[enters quietly and shyly, taps Monty on back]* Excuse me, aren't you Monty Mouth?
Monty:	Yes, I am! *[Leans down to Jimmy.]* Tell me, sonny, what are you waiting for?
Jimmy:	I've been waiting to grow up and be a newsman like you.
Monty:	Well, why wait? Here's your chance! *[Holds the microphone so that both of them can speak into it.]*
Jimmy:	This is Jimmy, your newsboy on the street, with a special interview with Mr. Monty Mouth. Mr. Mouth could you tell our TV audience what it is YOU are waiting for?
Monty:	I'd be glad to. I'm waiting for our Great God and Savior, Jesus Christ, to return as he promised.
Jimmy:	*[jumps up and down excitedly]* Me too! Me too!
Monty:	Ummm . . . Jimmy, the film is still rolling.
Jimmy:	Oh, OK! . . . This is Jimmy, your Christian newsboy on the street, signing off as we wait for Jesus. And now, back to our regularly scheduled program. *[Both exit.]*

Digging Deeper

What are some things that you wait for (want)?

What we are waiting for—what we want out of life—makes a difference in how we live. Can you think of some examples of that?

The Bible tells us, "The thing you should seek is God's kingdom. Then all the other things you need will be given to you" (Luke 12:31). What does this mean? How can we seek God's kingdom?

Don't Throw Stones

Scripture: 1 Samue…

Characters: Mike, S…

Mike: *[enters from left, c…* be late for school.

Sarah: *[enters from righ…*

Mike: Are you sick?

Sarah: No, I'm just not going to school.

Mike: Why?

Sarah: Because.

Mike: Because why?

Sarah: Because . . . because *[starts to cry]* because Kelsey said she was going to beat me up at recess today.

Mike: Why would Kelsey say something like that?

Sarah: She just doesn't like me. She always picks on me. Just because she is the tallest in my class, she thinks it's funny that I am the shortest.

Mike: What are you going to do?

Sarah: I'm not going to school ever again.

Mike: I don't think Mom and Dad will like that.

Sarah: Well, then, what do you think I should do?

Mike: Remember the story of David and Goliath? David was small and he was able to kill the giant because he trusted God.

Sarah: He killed the giant with a rock.

Mike:	Right, God protected David.
Sarah:	But the teacher says we can't throw rocks on the playground.
Mike:	No, Sarah, God doesn't want you to throw rocks at Kelsey. He wants you to believe that he will help you.
Sarah:	But what do I do about Kelsey?
Mike:	Well . . . *[pause]* I know! Why don't we pray for her?
Sarah:	I don't feel like praying for her.
Mike:	Come on, we'll pray together. *[Both bow heads.]* Dear God, please help Kelsey today. Help her to be kind. Show her that you love her. And, Lord, please help Sarah to be brave today at school. Amen.
Sarah:	Amen. Thanks for praying with me, Mike. I feel better.
Mike:	Hey, why don't you play with me at recess?
Sarah:	Can I?
Mike:	Sure!
Sarah:	Wow, Mike! David's big brothers didn't offer to help him! I think God is already answering my prayer!

Digging Deeper

What's the first thing you feel like doing when someone is mean to you? If Sarah had yelled at Kelsey, what do you think might have happened? Is it easy or hard to be quiet when someone is mean to you?

Mike wanted Sarah to know that she could be brave because God is on her side. God is always with us. Does that mean that we should go to dangerous places and pick fights with bullies?

When we do find ourselves in a dangerous situation, what should we do?

Power Machine

Scripture: Psalm 147:5

Characters: Rico, Kyle, one puppeteer to activate the "Power Machine"

Costumes/Props
- Cardboard box (Paint or draw gears and wheels and buttons on the sides to make it look like a machine.)
- Label the box with a sign that reads "POWER MACHINE."

Preparation
The cardboard box should be on stage before the puppets enter. Ask the audience to make motor sounds such as "Vroom" or other sounds when the box shakes. The slower it shakes, the softer the motor sounds should become. When the box stops shaking, the audience should stop their motor noises.

Script

The "Power Machine" is in the middle of the stage. Rico and Kyle enter from opposite sides of the stage.

Rico: Hey, Kyle, what's this?

Kyle: It's my fantastic new Power Machine. Pretty cool, huh?

Rico: What does it do?

Kyle: It has a double-barreled, fuel-injected, tuned-port, rocket engine.

Rico: Yeah, but what does it do?

Kyle: It runs at 15,000 RPMs and it has 3000 cubic inches of raw horsepower.

Rico: OK! OK! But what does it do?

Kyle: What does it do? Why, this baby is one powerful machine!

Rico: One last time—*[loudly]*—WHAT - DOES - IT - DO?

Kyle: What does it do? This Power Machine has all the knowledge of the entire universe stored in its memory banks.

Rico: Really?

Kyle: Want to see it run?

Rico: I sure do!

Kyle: Stand back 'cause this baby is powerful.

Rico moves back a little. Kyle pushes a button on the machine and the box shakes extra hard. Audience responds with motor noises. The box stops. Audience stops making noises.

Kyle: Hmmm, why did it stop? [Pushes button again.]

The box shakes less hard. Audience responds. The box stops. Audience stops. Kyle gives the box a hard whack. The box shakes slightly. Audience responds. Box stops. Audience stops.

Rico: [coming close to the box] What's wrong with it?

Kyle: I'm not sure.

Both look the machine over carefully.

Kyle: [looks around behind the box] Oh, here's the problem. I think the batteries are dead.

Rico: Batteries? Your all-powerful machine with all the knowledge of the universe runs on batteries?

Kyle: Yes, but, but . . . I can put new ones in right away. Wait till you hear it rumble!

Rico: No, thanks. I know where all the power and knowledge of the universe comes from. It comes from our all-powerful God, and he doesn't need batteries. See ya'!

Rico exits. Kyle exits, pushing the box ahead of him.

Digging Deeper

We have many wonderful machines and computers today that can do marvelous things. These inventions can make people feel very confident in their own abilities. Why can this be a problem?

Although computers can store far more information than a single human brain, they contain only the information that humans program into them. Since humans can never know all that God knows, can a computer ever know all that God knows?

Although scientists have discovered many wonderful things about human life and about the universe, they can never be "all-powerful." Only God can create something out of nothing. How many things can you name that God created out of nothing?

What is the difference between an invention and a creation?

I'm Hiding!

Scripture: Psalm 139:4-6

Characters: Tiki, Cody

Costumes/Props:
• Cut a lunch sack mask to fit over Tiki's head so that she can "see" out of the eyeholes.

Script

Tiki: *[enters with bag on her head, runs back and forth across stage stopping in the middle]* Oh, no! Oh, no! I have to find a place to hide!

Cody enters from the left, walks toward the middle of the stage.

Tiki: *[bumps into Cody]* OUCH! *[Whispers:]* Sorry, Cody.

Cody: Is . . . is . . . is that you, Tiki? *[Tries to see in the bag.]*

Tiki: SHH! *[Whispers:]* Yes, but keep it down!

Cody: What's with the paper bag? Did you have a bad hair day?

Tiki: Nooo! *[Whispers:]* I'm hiding.

Cody: You're hiding with a paper bag on your head?

Tiki: Yeah, so quiet it down!

Cody: Why are you hiding?

Tiki: *[in regular voice]* Well, do you promise not to tell?

Cody: Sure, I won't tell.

Tiki: Well, um . . . *[embarrassed]* I copied Allison's homework. Then I turned it in as my own.

Cody: Oh, that's not good.

Tiki: I know, that's why I'm hiding.

Cody: So, you're hiding from your teacher?

Tiki: My teacher? No, *[sighs]* she found out yesterday. I had to do the homework over.

Cody: Oh! So you're hiding from Mom and Dad?

Tiki: No, *[sadly]* they found out today. I'm grounded!

Cody: Well, then who are you hiding from?

Tiki: *[looks around to make sure no one is listening, then whispers]* God.

Cody: *[loudly]* GOD? You have a paper bag on your head because you are hiding from God?

Tiki: Yes, I'm hiding from God because I don't want him to know that I cheated.

Cody: Oh, Tiki, you can't hide from God.

Tiki: Well, I thought I was doing OK until you came along.

Cody: But Tiki, God knows everything. He is all around us all of the time.

Tiki: *[sadly]* You mean he saw me copying from Allison's paper?

Cody: Yes, he did. You can't hide anything from God. But you can ask him to forgive you.

Tiki: Oh. Ah . . . bye Cody! *[Starts to leave.]*

Cody: Hey, where are you going? *[Runs after her.]*

Tiki: To my room to pray—and throw this silly bag away. *[Both exit.]*

Digging Deeper

Because it's true that we can never hide from God, he can never "lose us" either. Why is this a good thing?

We might think that it is scary that God knows every single thing we've ever done. Why is this not a problem?

It's never a good idea to try to hide from God—or from anyone else in authority either. When we've done something wrong, what should we do next?

The Name Game

Scripture: Luke 2:1-20

Characters: Monty Mouth, Ryan, Olivia, one or two puppeteers for signs

Costumes/Props
- Microphone for Monty (lollipop with black tape or felt wrapped around it)
- Two cards for puppets to hold, "Jesus" and "God's Son"
- One cardboard tent sign that reads on one side "Jesus, the Son of God," and on the other side, "The Name Game"
- A sign on a stick to read "Applause"

Preparations
- "The Name Game" sign should be facing the audience in a prominent place on stage.
- The cards "Jesus" and "God's Son" should be backstage ready to attach to the contestants' hands.
- Ask the audience to respond to applause sign.

Script

Monty Mouth enters with microphone. Ryan enters from right. Olivia enters from the left.

Monty: Welcome to our holiday special of "The Name Game." We have with us two contestants ready to match their wits against "The Name Game Board." *[Turns to Ryan, then to Olivia.]* This is Ryan on the right and Olivia on the left. Welcome to "The Name Game."

Sign: Applause; audience responds. *[Sign exits.]*

Monty: Before we begin, let me go over the rules for our listening audience. I will give each contestant three clues to the name that is covered on the board. *[Points to sign.]* Each one may ask one question after each clue. Then each one will be given an opportunity to guess *[with lots of emotion]* "The Name Game Name!" Let's hear it for our contestants. Yea!

Sign: Applause; audience responds. *[Sign exits.]*

Monty: Ready, contestants?

Both: Ready!

Monty: Olivia, your first clue is . . . "Prince of Peace."

Olivia:	OK . . . um . . . did he float down the Nile in a basket?
Monty:	No, but you're right in thinking that Moses was a prince, and he did bring peace. But Moses is not the name we're looking for—sorry. Ryan, the next clue is, "The Good Shepherd."
Ryan:	Let's see . . . did he kill a giant?
Monty:	No, Ryan, but you're right—David was a good shepherd and he did kill a giant. But "David" is not the name we're looking for. Back to Olivia with the next clue which is "Immanuel."
Olivia:	Oh! Oh! Was he from the family of David?
Monty:	Yes, he was! Good question! Ryan, here is your clue: "Messiah."
Ryan:	Messiah . . . Was he from Nazareth?
Monty:	Yes! [to audience] It looks like our contestants are on the right track! Olivia, here's your final clue . . . "Redeemer."
Olivia:	Monty, did angels announce his birth?
Monty:	Correct! Well done, Olivia! All right, Ryan, this is the last and final clue of the game. After your question, you and Olivia will be sent backstage to make your decisions. And here is the clue: "Savior."
Ryan:	Oh, I think I might know. Was he born in a stable?
Monty:	Amazing! We have another "yes" answer! . . . Well, that's it, contestants, time to write your answers. Good luck!

Ryan and Olivia exit. Behind stage attach the "Jesus" card to Olivia's hand and the "God's Son" card to Ryan's hand.

Monty:	[speaks to audience] What do you think? Will our contestants come up with the correct name? Remember, the clues were "Prince of Peace, The Good Shepherd, Immanuel, Messiah, Redeemer, and Savior." Here come our contestants now.

Ryan and Olivia enter with cards.

Monty:	Olivia, show us your card. [Olivia holds up "Jesus" card.] Jesus!
Sign:	Applause; audience responds. [Sign exits.]

Monty: And Ryan what is your answer? *[Ryan holds up "God's Son" card.]* God's Son!

Sign: Applause; audience responds. *[Sign exits.]*

Puppeteer turns around the "Name Game" board to show "Jesus, the Son of God."

Monty: We are making game show history here today, folks! For the first time, we have two winners. The answer is "Jesus, the Son of God!" Both of our contestants will win an all-expense paid trip to Bethlehem!

Sign: Applause. All exit jumping and cheering.

Digging Deeper

One of the most exciting facts about the Bible is the record it contains of all the prophecies made about Jesus hundreds of years before his birth. To find where Jesus was called "Immanuel" and "Prince of Peace," look up Isaiah 7:14 and Isaiah 9:6.

We often refer to "Jesus Christ" as though "Christ" is Jesus' last name. But "Christ" is one of Jesus' titles. To find out what it means, look up John 1:41 and John 4:25.

We often call Jesus our Good Shepherd. To find out why, look up John 10:11 and 14.

Prayer-Athon

Scripture: Luke 11:1-13

Characters: Monty Mouth, Buster, Iwanna, Hope, one puppeteer for signs

Costumes/Props:
- Microphone for Monty (cover a lollipop with black tape or felt)
- Long paper for Iwanna's list
- "Applause" sign
- "No Way" sign

Preparation
- Ask the audience to respond to the signs when they appear.

Script

Monty Mouth enters with microphone in hand.

Monty: This is Monty Mouth coming to you from channel P-R-A-Y with our annual Prayer-Athon. Contestants are challenged to pray in the manner that Jesus taught us to pray. Our studio audience will be voting with their applause after each contestant. And you at home may vote by calling our toll-free number, 1-800-LUKE-11-1-13 . . . That's 1-800-LUKE-11-1-13. And now for our first contestant all the way from Revenge, Nevada. Let's have a big welcome for contestant number one: Buster!

Sign: Applause; audience responds. *[Sign exits.]*

Buster: *[enters and greets emcee]* Howdy, Monty! I'm here to pray.

Monty: Pray away, Buster. *[Moves to side of stage whenever contestants pray.]*

Buster: *[looks up to Heaven, speaks loudly]* Hey, God! I've got this person I want to talk to you about. Jake broke my remote control car. So now, God . . . I want you to break his head! Amen! . . . *[Turns to Monty.]* That's it, Monty.

Monty: *[raises his hands in surprise]* Well, if that's it, I guess that's it. *[Turns to audience.]* Audience, it's time to vote.

Sign: No Way; audience responds. *[Sign exits.]*

Buster exits, grumbling loudly.

Monty: Well . . . ahem . . . Now for our next contestant who is here from Greed, California. Let's hear it for Iwanna!

Sign: Applause; audience responds. *[Sign exits.]*

Iwanna: *[acts impatient and talks fast, enters with list in hand]* I wanna pray right now! *[Holds up list.]* OK, God, here's my list. I wanna a pony, I wanna CD player. I wanna go-cart. I wanna dirt bike. I wanna go to Sea World and anything else you want to give me. Amen. Oh, oh, and I want it all right away. Amen again. OK, Monty, I'm done for now.

Monty: *[shakes head sadly]* Oh, my, ah, well . . . thanks . . . Um, audience that was contestant number two. It's time to vote.

Sign: No Way; audience responds. *[Sign exits.]*

Iwanna exits, loudly adding things to her list.

Monty: Hmmm . . . Now for our third and final contestant who comes to us from Humble, Missouri: Miss Hope! Yea!!

Sign: Applause; audience responds. *[Sign exits.]*

Hope: *[enters shyly, turns toward audience]* Oh, thank you, thank you. *[Faces Monty.]* Thank you, Mr. Mouth. Excuse me, sir, would you like me to pray now?

Monty: Whenever you're ready, Miss Hope.

Hope: *[puts hands together and bows head, speaks clearly and slowly]* Dear Father, I praise your name. I want you to have your way in my life, Lord. Thank you for giving me what I need every day. Please forgive me for all of the wrong things I do, and help me to forgive others. Lord, help me to make wise choices when I am tempted, and protect me from evil. Thank you for hearing my prayer, Lord. I love you. In Jesus' name, amen.

Sign: Applause; audience responds. *[Sign exits.]*

Monty: *[comes forward to congratulate Miss Hope]* Wow! Miss Hope's prayer came right from the heart. Now that's the way Jesus taught us to pray. Don't you agree, audience?

Sign: Applause; audience responds. *[Sign exits.]*

Monty: Way to pray, Miss Hope! Well, that about wraps it up for another year. This is Monty Mouth from channel P-R-A-Y, signing off. *[Turns to Hope:]* Say, Miss Hope, would you mind praying for me?

Both exit.

Digging Deeper

Monty's toll-free number was 1- 800-LUKE 11-1-13. That's too many numbers for a phone number, but it's just right for learning how to pray. Look up Luke 11:1-13 and see how many directions you can find for how to pray.

Prayer is one of the most special privileges and honors we have in life. Why is that?

Monty said Miss Hope's prayer came "right from the heart." What does that mean? Why is it important to be honest with God when we pray?

We Can't Compete

Scripture: Mark 4:35-41

Characters: Megan, Kevin, one puppeteer to manipulate tree

Costumes/Props:
• Modern clothing
• Extension cord
• Two trees cut from cardboard, one with a stick taped to its back

Preparation

Tape one tree on its side as if it has blown over on the left of the stage.
A puppeteer should hold the other tree upright on the right of the stage.
Attach the electric extension cord to Megan's hand.
Ask the audience to try to blow the upright tree over when the tree begins to shake.

Script

Megan and Kevin enter from the right. Megan has an electric cord in her hand. They walk across stage and look at the tree that has been blown over.

Megan: Hey, Kevin, look at this! *[Points to the downed tree.]*

Kevin: Wow! It must have blown over in last night's storm.

Megan: That was some storm all right, and just in time, too!

Kevin: What do you mean?

Megan: Well, I needed an idea for the school science fair. Now, I have one.

Kevin: If you're going to try to make it storm, I'm out of here! *[Starts to leave.]*

Megan: No, wait! I can't make it storm. But see this electric extension cord?

Kevin: Yeah. What's it for?

Megan: I have it plugged into 25 powerful, industrial fans. I'm going to see how much wind it will take to blow over this other tree.

Kevin: Wow! That's cool! Can I watch?

Megan: Sure! But we better take cover when I plug in this cord.

Kevin: Yeah, right! We don't want to be blown into the next county.

Megan and Kevin exit.

Megan: *[from offstage]* Hang on! Here goes!

Tree begins to shake slightly. Audience responds by blowing at tree. As audience blows, tree shakes more, then starts to lean a little. Tree struggles against the "wind" and remains upright. Tree stops shaking. Audience stops blowing. Megan and Kevin return.

Megan: *[looks at tree]* That tree sure has some strong roots.

Kevin: I'll say.

Megan: Maybe I need more fans.

Kevin: Maybe you need a new science project.

Megan: What do you mean?

Kevin: Well, the Bible says that Jesus is the only one who has power over nature.

Megan: Oh, yeah! He made the wind and the waves calm down—I remember now.

Kevin: And he doesn't have to use an electric cord.

Megan and Kevin start to exit.

Megan: Hey, if I got a bunch of ice, maybe I could use these fans to make a blizzard!

Kevin: *[shaking head]* Oh, no! Here we go again!

Digging Deeper

Do you know why Jesus has power over nature? To find out, look up Colossians 1:15-17 and John 1:1-4 ("The Word" is Jesus).

Since Jesus has power over nature, why do we still have tornadoes, earthquakes, and floods?

Scientists have learned how to predict where a storm will go, and when a volcano will erupt, and can even give us some warning for an earthquake, but will they ever be able to control these things?

The One True God

Scripture: Daniel 6

Characters: Matt, Brett, three puppeteers for the signs

Costumes/Props
- Sunglasses for puppets or pompoms
- Signs to read: "No!" and "The Lord is God" and "The One True God"

Preparation
- This script may be done as a cheer or a rap. Dress puppets accordingly.
- Ask audience to respond when the signs are shown.

——— Script ———

Matt and Brett enter.

Matt: *[points to Brett]* Hi! He's Brett!

Brett: *[points to Matt]* And his name's Matt!

Both: And we're here to tell you
Just where it's at!

Matt: There's one true God;
　　He's the God we serve.
You can read about him
　　In his holy Word.

Brett: You know, Daniel was thrown
　　Into the lions' den
For praying to the Lord,
　　And bowing down to him.

But the one thing the king
　　Didn't know that night
Was the one true God
　　Shut up the lions' bite.

Matt: Shadrach, Meshach,
　　Abednego, too,
Would not bow down
　　To the king's statue.

"If you don't," said the king,
    "I'll throw you in the furnace."
"Well, we won't," said the boys,
    "So you'll have to burn us."

The Lord God met them
    In the fire, no joke.
And when the king called 'em out,
    They didn't smell like smoke.

Brett: So, you see, their king
    And Daniel's king, too,
Found there's only one God,
    Only one that's true.

Matt: We must love him far more
    Than any other thing;
He's the one true God,
    Our Lord and King.

Brett: Tell me, who is God?

Sign: "The Lord is God"; audience responds. *[Sign exits.]*

Matt: And who's our God?

Sign: "The One True God"; audience responds. *[Sign exits.]*

Brett: Is money our God?

Signs: "No!" and "The Lord is God"; audience responds. *[Signs exits.]*

Matt: Are sports our God?

Signs: "No!" and "The Lord is God"; audience responds. *[Signs exits.]*

Brett: Are clothes our God?

Signs: "No!" and "The Lord is God"; audience responds. *[Signs exits.]*

Both: The Lord our God is the one true God!

Both bow and exit.

Digging Deeper

The first of the Ten Commandments is "You must not have any other gods except me." Because God is God, he has every right to command us to worship no one or nothing else. What other things, or people, can become so important to us that we want them more than we want God?

How can you know when something is beginning to become a god to you?

Because God is God, we must respect him and honor him. What are some ways we can do this?

Good Friday, Good News

Scripture: Mark 14, 15

Characters: Jeff, Jaynie, Jim

Costumes/Props
• Attach a tissue to one of Jaynie's hands.

Script

Jaynie enters, wiping her eyes and sniffing. Jim and Jeff enter.

Jeff: Hey, Jaynie, what's the matter?

Jaynie: What's the matter? *[Louder]* WHAT'S THE MATTER? I'll tell you what's the matter; I am having a very BAD DAY!

Jim: You are? Why don't you tell us about it?

Jaynie: Well, first of all, I got up super early and worked three hours on my homework. I had it perfect. Then, on the way to school, I dropped it in the mud. The teacher said she couldn't even read it, so I had to miss recess to write it over. Then during the spelling test, I dropped my pencil. When I leaned over to get it, Joe stepped on my fingers. It hurt so bad I screamed and Mrs. Waddle made me write my name on the board. The chalk dust made me sneeze and everybody laughed. It was a Very Bad Day!

Jim: I'm sorry that you had such a bad day, but remember, today is GOOD Friday and that should cheer you up.

Jaynie: *[sighs, speaks in a sad voice]* Isn't this the day that Jesus died?

Jim: Of course it is! That's what makes it Good Friday.

Jaynie: *[still sad]* Well, what's so good about that?

Jeff: Come to think of it . . . that sounds more like Bad Friday.

Jaynie: Yeah, *[sigh]* what's so good about Good Friday?

Jim: It's good because Jesus died on the cross for us.

Jaynie: That makes me so sad.

Jeff: Yeah, me, too.

Jim: But it's good.

Jaynie: How can that be good?

Jim: Because Jesus died to take away our sins. That's the Good News of Good Friday!

Jaynie: Jesus died because of our sins?

Jeff: That sounds like Bad News to me!

Jim: It sounds that way until you've heard the REALLY GOOD NEWS!

Jeff: The REALLY Good News?

Jaynie: *[more cheerful]* I remember now . . . it's that Jesus died and took away all our sins. But he didn't stay in the grave!

Jeff: Oh, that's right! He rose again on Easter morning.

Jim: Right, that's the Good News!

Jaynie: *[very cheerful]* So, it is a Good Friday!

Jeff: It is a very Good Friday!

Digging Deeper

Although it's hard to think of Jesus' death as a good thing, it is, in fact, the best thing that's ever happened for us. Why is that true?

We might feel sorry for Jesus if we thought God forced him to die for our sins. But the truth is that Jesus chose to pay that awful price for our sins. Why did Jesus do this?

Good Friday gets even better because of Sunday morning. What happened then? How do we remember and celebrate Good Friday during every Sunday worship service?

Treasure Map

Scripture: John 3:16, 17

Characters: Tyrone, Tess

Costumes/Props:
- Modern clothing
- Treasure map with corner clearly torn off
- The torn-off corner of the map
- Cardboard street signs: "Prayer Street" and "Good Deeds Avenue"

Preparation
Attach treasure map to one of Tyrone's hands. Attach the torn-off corner to one of Tess's hands. Street signs should be in place on stage before puppets enter.

Script

Tyrone enters carrying treasure map. He wanders back and forth across stage, acting confused and lost.

Tyrone: Let's see. *[Looks at street sign.]* How did I get here? I thought I was at Obey Street. Well, I guess if I backtrack, I'll see where I went wrong.

Starts backing up and bumps into Tess who has entered from right. Tess has a small piece of paper in hand.

Both: Oops! Sorry!

Tess: Hi, Tyrone! What have you got there?

Tyrone: This is an eternal treasure map, but I just can't seem to make sense of it!

Tess: Let me see where you are. *[Looks at map Tyrone is holding.]*

Tyrone: I'll tell you where I am, I'm lost!

Tess: Well, no wonder you're lost, look at your map!

Tyrone: But that's what I have been doing, looking at this map! *[Shakes map.]*

Tess: *[points to map]* Right here's your problem. You have a piece missing, and it's the most important part of the map.

Tyrone:	It is?
Tess:	Yes, it is. No wonder, you're lost. The place to start on this map is gone. You were trying to start in the middle of the map.
Tyrone:	I was?
Tess:	Yes, these streets, Prayer and Good Deeds, don't make sense unless you start at the beginning.
Tyrone:	But you said the beginning of the map is missing. Now, I'll never find the eternal treasure.
Tess:	Oh, yes, you will, because I found the piece of your map that's missing.
Tyrone:	You did? Let me see it.
Tess:	*[holds up piece of map for Tyrone]* Look, it's right here. It says, "Begin by asking Jesus to be your Lord and Savior."
Tyrone:	Let's go back to the beginning and start with him.
Tess:	Good idea.

Digging Deeper

When people try to do things or go places without following the directions, what usually happens?

Do you think God gave us clear directions on how to find our "eternal treasure"?

There are many steps along the way to Heaven. As Tess said, you must "begin by asking Jesus to be your Lord and Savior." What are some of the other steps? Can you take a wrong direction once you get started? If so, what should you do then?

Lost and Found

Scripture: Luke 15

Characters: Levi, Casey, one puppeteer to manipulate the box

Costumes/Props:
- Cut the top and bottom out of two cardboard boxes so that the puppets can appear to be sitting in the boxes.
- Label one box "Found."
- Label the other box "Lost" on one side and "Found" on the opposite side.

Preparation:
The "Found" box should be attached to the stage in a manner that allows Levi to come through the bottom and appear to be inside. Casey will be inside the "Lost" and "Found" box with the "Lost" sign toward the audience. Later, the box will be turned to show the "Found" label.

Script

Both boxes on stage. Levi is in the "Found" box. Casey is in the "Lost" box. Levi hums "Jesus Loves Me" happily.

Casey: *[sighs sadly, looks over at Levi]* Look at Levi over in that "Found" box. I wonder if I'll ever be found. It seems like I've been lost my whole life. *[Hangs head.]*

Levi: *[full of joy!]* Boy, is it great to be found!

Casey: *[big sigh]* I've tried everything to be found. I got a new haircut so that I would look beautiful . . . But no one claimed me. *[Hangs head.]*

Levi: *[filled with joy]* Praise the Lord! I've been found!

Casey: *[looks over at Levi with a big sigh]* I got all "A's" on my grade card . . . But no one claimed me. *[Hangs head.]*

Levi: *[shouts]* HALLELUJAH!

Casey: *[jumps when Levi shouts, then sighs a big sigh. She hits her head on the box several times, then looks back up.]* I even got the lead role in our school play, but . . . no one claimed me.

Levi: *[with great joy]* I'm so glad to be found!

Casey: *[looks over at Levi, speaks disgustedly]* Hey, do you think you could hold it down a little over there? Not everybody has been found, you know.

Levi: *[looks over at Casey]* Oh! I guess I got a little carried away. It just feels soooo good to be found!

Casey: Yes, I gathered that. *[Turns head away in disgust.]*

Levi: I'm sorry. I remember what it was like to be lost.

Casey: *[turns back to look at Levi, still speaks disgustedly]* Well, if it's not too much bother, could you tell me the secret?

Levi: It's no secret, Casey. It's Jesus.

Casey: Jesus? *[Sadly]* Why would he want to claim me?

Levi: Because he loves you!

Casey: Then why hasn't he claimed me?

Levi: He is waiting for you to ask him!

Casey: OH! *[Pause.]* Levi, will you pray with me? *[Both bow heads.]* Dear Lord Jesus, I want to be claimed by you. Show me how to follow you for the rest of my life so that I won't ever be lost again. Thank you for loving me. Amen.

Levi: Amen!

Puppeteer turns box slowly as Casey is praying so that the "Found" label can be read by the audience.

Both: *[shout]* HALLELUJAH!

Digging Deeper

It took Levi a long time to notice Casey's unhappiness. Do you think we are sometimes like that? How can we learn to be more sensitive to others?

Jesus told many stories about things or people that were lost, and how someone searched for them. Three of those stories are found in Luke 15. What was lost in these stories, and who did the looking?

In each of these stories, the lost thing or person represents us. Who is it who loves us and is looking for us? Does God force us to come to him?

Holey, Holey, Holey

Scripture: 1 Peter 1:15

Characters: Joy, Adam, Josh

Costumes/Props:
- Shirt for Josh with lots of holes cut into it (See appendix for pattern.)

Script

Adam and Joy enter from opposite sides of stage.

Joy: Adam, have you seen my Sunday shoes?

Adam: No, have you seen my blue tie?

Joy: No, sorry. *[Calls to brother off stage:]* Josh!

Josh: *[enters from right, wearing holey shirt]* OK! OK! I'm ready!

Joy: *[looks at shirt]* Good grief, Josh, what happened to your shirt?

Josh: Do you like it? It's my new Sunday school shirt. I made it myself! *[Turns around to show off shirt.]*

Adam: *[points at shirt]* You can't wear that to church!

Josh: I most certainly can; that's what I made it for!

Joy: Josh, you made that shirt?

Josh: I sure did!

Adam: But it's all full of holes!

Josh: You've got it! It's my holey shirt.

Adam: Your holey shirt?

Joy: You mean you put holes in it on purpose?

Josh: Right, because Pastor _____ said that the Bible tells us to be holey because God is holey.

Adam: But Josh, being holy doesn't mean being full of holes!

Josh: HUH?

Joy: Josh, when the Bible says to be holy, it means to be more like God.

Josh: But I can't be like God. After all, God is . . . well . . . GOD!

Adam: Yes, but we can try every day to do what he wants us to do. And when we accept Jesus as our Savior, God sends his Holy Spirit to help us.

Joy: So you see, Josh, being holy means something very different from wearing holey clothes.

Josh: Oh! I think I get it. Wearing a holey shirt doesn't make me HOLY! So—I guess it's OK if I don't wear this shirt to church?

Adam: It's very OK!

Josh: Good! 'Cause I was starting to feel a breeze! BR-R-R!

All exit.

Digging Deeper

It's important that we understand how to be holy, because Peter told us that we are to "be holy in all that you do, just as God is holy" (1 Peter 1:15). What does this mean? Can we ever be like God? What are we supposed to do?

Adam told Josh that "when we accept Jesus as our Savior, God sends his Holy Spirit to help us." Have you ever felt God's Holy Spirit helping you? When a bad idea pops into your head, and then you think, No, I shouldn't do that, who do you think is telling you that? Has God's Holy Spirit ever prompted you to go do something nice for someone?

A Tale of Two Ladies

Scripture: Philippians 2:1-4

Characters: Mandy, Tyler, Molly, one older child or adult with an authoritative voice to narrate from behind or beside the stage

Costumes/Props
- Three small white cards for grade cards, one attached to the hand of each puppet
- A sign reading "The End"

Script

Narrator speaks from behind or beside the stage

Narrator: When grade cards come out at your school, do you compare grades with your friends? Do you think there is a right way and a wrong way to act when this happens? Let's watch and listen, and see what we can learn.

Mandy and Tyler enter from opposite sides and meet in the middle.

Mandy: Hey Tyler, I see you got your grade card. What did you get in math?

Tyler: Let's see . . . *[Looks at card.]* I got a "B."

Mandy: *[full of pride]* Well, I got an "A+!" What did you get in science?

Tyler: Umm, well . . . science isn't my best subject. I got a . . . "C-."

Mandy: *[bragging]* That's too bad. I got all "A's." But then, my daddy said brains run in our family. Isn't that great?

Tyler stands with his head down as Mandy exits and Molly enters.

Molly: Hi, Tyler!

Tyler: *[sadly, with head down]* Oh, hi, Molly.

Molly: Are you OK?

Tyler: Not really. Here, see for yourself. *[Holds the card for Molly to see.]*

Molly: *[kindly]* Tyler, that's a good card! Look, you did better than I did in math. *[Holds up her card.]*

Tyler:	But look at my science grade.
Molly:	Yes, but isn't that better than you got on your last card?
Tyler:	*[encouraged]* Yeah, it is better! I guess you're right!
Molly:	And look how well you did in art and music!
Tyler:	But those are easy subjects!
Mandy:	Not to me! They're easy for you because you're good at them.
Tyler:	*[happily]* Molly, do you know what you're good at?
Molly:	What?
Tyler:	You're good at being a friend. *[They exit together.]*
Narrator:	Now I ask you, which of these two girls acted in a loving way to Tyler?
Sign:	"The End."

Digging Deeper

Let's answer the narrator's question: who was the better friend to Tyler? Why?

When you get better grades than others, or are better at sports, or have talents that they don't have, are you tempted to think that you are a better person than they are? What can we do when we feel that way?

Who gave us the brains, body, and ability that we have? Who helped us develop those talents? Instead of feeling proud, do you think we should feel grateful?

EVERYONE has some kind of gift from God. Some people, like Mandy, are good at making others feel better. Some people are good at singing, or playing an instrument. Some people are really good at sharing what they have. What other kinds of gifts does God give people? Think about the people sitting around you; what gifts do they have?

Appendix

No-Sew Easy Puppet Costume Pattern

1. Enlarge pattern to fit puppet.
2. Fold material at neckline.
3. Cut on three sides (bold lines). Do not cut on the fold.
4. Cut neck opening and front opening as marked by broken line.
5. (Optional) Use safety pins to hold the sides together, or cut a strip of material to be used as a belt.

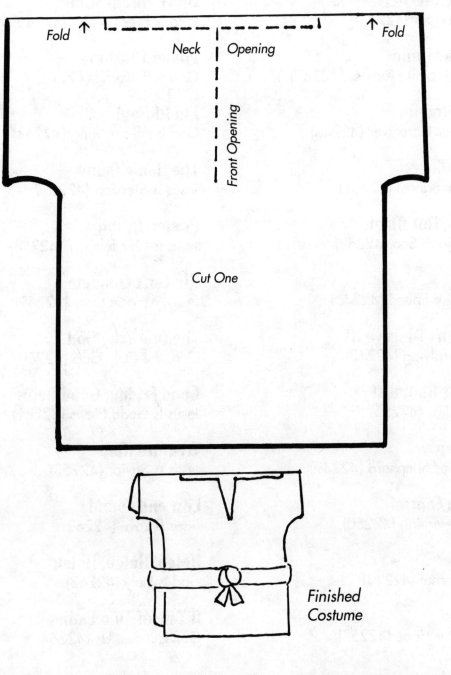

Fold

Fold

Neck   Opening

Front Opening

Cut One

Finished
Costume

Worship Resources

Each of the skits in this book correlates to a unit of worship from Standard Publishing's two-year series of Worship Folders for elementary kids. This series was developed to help children worship God for who he is and what he has done. Each eight-page folder is a thematic unit with Scripture activities, music, prayer suggestions, and small group ideas for four sessions of children's worship.

Listed with each skit title below is the correlating Worship Folder and its order number.

Counting the Stars
God Is Creator (42241)

Headlight Smile
God Is a Promise Keeper (42247)

Bag of Worries
God Is Our Caregiver (42248)

Sheep Talk
Jesus Is Immanuel (42251)

Miracles, Not Magic
Jesus Is God's Son (42252)

Far Out!
Jesus Is Our Friend (42246)

She Doesn't Deserve It!
God Is Forgiving (42243)

No Doubt About It!
Jesus Is Alive (42255)

Fair Sheep
Jesus Is Our Shepherd (42249)

God Is in Control
God Is Sovereign (42250)

"E-Turtle?"
God Is Eternal (42244)

Waiting
Jesus Is Our Hope (42256)

Don't Throw Stones
God Is Ever-Present (42245)

Power Machine
God Is Powerful (42242)

I'm Hiding!
God Is All-Knowing (42254)

The Name Game
Jesus Is Messiah (42257)

Prayer-Athon
Jesus Is Our Teacher (42258)

We Can't Compete
Jesus, Miracle Doer (42259)

The One True God
God, the Only God (42260)

Good Friday, Good News
Jesus Is Good News (42261)

Treasure Map
Jesus Is Savior (42253)

Lost and Found
Jesus Is Love (42262)

Holey, Holey, Holey
God Is Holy (42263)

A Tale of Two Ladies
God Is Inside Us (42264